Life Poetically Embraced

R. Queen

Fulton Books, Inc.
Meadville, PA

Published by Fulton Books 2021

ISBN 978-1-63860-243-9 (paperback)
ISBN 978-1-63860-244-6 (digital)

Printed in the United States of America

Dedicated with an abundance of thanks to Vera, Jackie Faye, Carrie D., Juanita M., Linda A., M. Johnson, my GH crew, my husband and family.

All of you in some way helped me stop ignoring the elephant in the room, to address it, and have the ability to embrace it.

Now and Laters
and
Bubble Gum

It started with a smile or a shy "hello," and for one generation, it was "bubble gum," and "now and laters" that created friends as well as haters. The ones who wanted some but didn't get any.

If you had candy, you were cool and had friends to walk home with after school.

Not much to worry about at all, except who sat by you and if the person you liked, liked you too.

We all grew up, and life got real. Kids, marriages, divorces, bad relationships, successes, failures, and paying bills.

As you go, you learn of those who appreciate and of those who annihilate and manipulate.

Things in life go from easy to hard, to satisfying, to misleading and troublesome, and to irritating and thinking you may never overcome.

Things can make you want to complain or even feel you may go insane. You look for understanding when things become so demanding.

One day, it all becomes clear. All you have to do is be sincere (be true to yourself). Knowing who you are after the pain has left its scar. You realize that you are stronger.

Why this and why that, you question no longer.

Things change and time goes on. It will never be as simple as "now and laters" and "bubble gum."

Life is too short, so appreciate where you've been and where you came from.

A Plan in Place

Peering out the window, noticing branches on trees swaying in the
wind
Sunlight creating sparkles on vehicles parked nearby
Such a beautiful day or so I thought
I opened the front door and was slapped with humidity
Oh, the deception of the view is now being felt in the worst way
Proving that sometimes looks can be deceiving
Just like people, you can let them suck the life out of you, or take a
step back to get a plan in place
Get ahead of their stupidity and
Walk away with grace and dignity

It's Not Always the Way It Seems

Sometimes things get rough, and you deal with them the best way
you know how. And it seems that's still not enough.

A bottomless pit is where you may fall, or you have a mountain to
climb that seems way too tall

What is this that keeps making us feel defeated, unimportant, and
not needed?

Things that we have no control over can get the best of us, make us
feel alone, and not sure who to trust.

In everything, there is a lesson to be learned, so really there is no need
to be concerned.

Everything you go through becomes a part of you. The lesson(s) you
learn may not had been just for you, but for someone who may
come into your life at a time when things are going right.

Headache and Heartbreak

My head aches, my heart breaks
How could it all had been a mistake or was it not?
How can being there one hundred percent not produce a love that makes it time well spent?
How is it possible that one person can give their all, and the other be mostly blind to it all?
At one time, there was the enjoyment of anticipating what the next day may bring, whether it was a simple smile, an unexpected thank you, or learning something new about the person that made you feel good inside.
Now, it seems strange because the thrill is mostly gone, and you feel alone.
Has the passion you once had really died?
So many questions but not many answers.
It leaves you with a pain in your soul and tears in your eyes.
All you ever wanted was to be happy and hold the one you love near, not feel sad with every memory that brings a tear.
As you reminisce, you wonder how did it come to this.
When did it start to go wrong?
You were true from the start, so you've done your part.
Your life is more than a sad love song.

Don't Blame It on Being Drunk

You forced yourself on me while I was trying to sleep
There is no way this marriage will keep
You say it's because you were drunk, like it's a myth you are daring
    someone to debunk
Too heavy for me to move
In that moment, for you, my body does not call
Trapped under you, I try to fight, but I am just way too small
My body feels no intimacy, in its place there's a sign that says vacancy
Selfishness and arrogance is fueling your mind
Searching for some super strength that I just cannot find
No matter how hard I try, you just ignore my cry
Your drinking clouded your thinking, you say
It wasn't that cloudy since you remembered it all the very next day
Too heavy for me to move
In court you lie, making it harder for me to prove
Basking in your lawyer's grace with that sneaky grin on your face
I don't think you will ever comprehend what you stole from me
This marriage has fallen deep between the cracks
Looking forward to getting back what makes me, me
You don't get to keep that
After years of walking on eggshells and trying to please you
I can finally say I'm through.

I Refuse

Being afraid to even just say one word,
I'm here screaming on the inside, so much hurt and nothing to stop
the pain.
Being stripped of everything that once was me.
Forced to stay down and not make a sound.
Not sure what to do, will my words be heard?
So tired of feeling like I'm stuck in a dark pit, and so tired of all the
bullshi——
I find a little courage, only to be knocked back down,
Not holding on to that anymore, have to pick myself up and rise high
above the floor.
I've come to it, and now, I'm making my way through it.
My spirit maybe broken and bruised, my faith weakened but letting
this define me.
I refuse.

Ready to Take It On

Concerned and worried a lot,
A cough that hurts your chest and makes it hard to rest.
You've never smoked, though you tried it once and felt dizzy.
In that moment, you said to yourself, "This isn't for me."

Many times, it was hard to avoid secondhand smoke, now you learn
    there is a thirdhand smoke. This stuff is no joke.
On the curtains, toys, and so much more
Lurking on the back of the door and settled in clothes.
All you were doing was breathing with your nose.

The doctor speculates lung cancer, you hope that's the wrong answer.
Now, on the way to chest X-ray.
Will it show a cancerous mass?
To which you'd say, "No thanks, I'll pass," (as if you have a choice).

So many tests, blood drawn, and in a cup, you must pee while ques-
    tioning, "why is this happening to me?"
In your moment of wonder and wait, you think of other things it
    could be and of all the things you appreciate.

You start thinking back, where did it originate? The small apartment
    you lived in some time ago? Could this had been the place of
    doom with its yellow tinged walls and carpet in every room?
    The smell of smoke down every hall?
Stress builds as you await the doctor's call. Whatever it may be, you've
    gotten yourself ready to take it on.

Biopsy Done

Biopsy done
Waiting has begun
Options given, just incase
Two weeks out, what will the results reveal
Worst possible scenarios starting to set in
Should I prepare for the worst
Just one more week for the answers I seek
One questionable test started my mind's unrest
Results now in, no cancer
Wait a minute
Only got five seconds of joy
Now, surgery is what they want to deploy
It's a preventative measure, they say
Hoping positivity finds its way
My heart and mind seem to form a knot
Fear and worry are pulling at me a lot

Time to Move On

The place you call home should be welcoming.
As you approach, it should be the place you feel safe so excited to be
    almost there.

In time, it became a part of you. In every room, there is a story and
    many memories you hope to always hold on to.
Then, something terrible happens and ruined all the good it once
    represented.
You can no longer see yourself in it.
It had become a dreadful place, all the stories and memories, now
    you hope and wish you could erase.
A negative energy has contaminated every space.

A home to you, it is no longer.
The entrance is now a portal to unpleasant reminders.
Time to move on, no longer a pawn in someone's game.
This season has come to an end.

Safety Zone

Afraid to venture out to see what life may bring about.
In there, it's just you.
You are comfortable there.

When others try to come in, you keep them out.
Afraid they may corrupt your space.
In there, it's only supposed to be you.
This is your safe space.
It may be lonely at times, but you still keep those away who keep
    trying to change your mind.

This is your safety zone, so why won't they just leave you alone?
You try to step out a little bit, a few one hundred feet.
Once you realize there is a chance for commitment (relationships,
    jobs, etc.), or just to be a part of a group or something bigger
    than you, back to the safety zone you retreat.
Afraid of disappointment, hurt, or making a mistake, you make every
    excuse why you can't.
You don't want to leave your space. In there, you go at your own pace.

Shielding yourself from everything is not living.
It's okay to be cautious about what others are giving, but don't ana-
    lyze everything; doing so is very exhausting.
So take a little chance, here and there.
Live in the moment, no more excuses.
In your mind, you are keeping your safe place on standby.
Stop limiting yourself and reveal what you have to offer to you.

You Will Shine Through

It's hard to see beauty in anything, and to remember you're strong
when someone is constantly tearing you down and doing you
wrong.

Where is the beauty in feeling insignificant? Where is the strength
when you feel weak, trapped, and emotionally drained?

What can you do when you think you've lost all that makes you, you?
When you feel like you're on a roller coaster that seems to never
come to a stop? With way too many ups and downs.

You want off this ride, it's really hurting your pride. With tears
streaming down your face, you hope for love, but everything
appears to be moving at a snail's pace.

You look in the mirror and see someone you don't recognize, with
so much suffering and hurt in your eyes. There has to be some-
thing you can do. You get up and fight, and all that is you will
shine through.

An Unclear Mind

Cloudy mind, no assessment of time.
Driven by confusion, progressing nowhere.
Holding steady in limbo.

A clear path in any direction, the mind does not show.
This isn't uncharted territory, so why does it seem like a new story?
How and why are the same questions that are always asked while
    waiting for clarity to be unmasked?

In Search of Me

Feeling hidden, lost, and out of place.
Where am I? Who am I? Where is me? Who is me?
Confusion has taken up lots of space.
I once was here. I once was me.
Now, unrecognizable on the inside, presenting an illusion on the
outside.
Don't think anyone notices as I wonder, am I good enough?
I don't have what they have or what they want.
Giving all I've got has to be enough.
In search of a moment of peace, just to search for me.
Even a glimpse seems hard to find in this jumbled up mind.
Where am I? Who am I? Where is me? Who is me?
I once knew.

The Ride

On the road, it all suddenly became clear, things that once were are
    left behind.
No more confusion or uncertainty.
The road brings much clarity.
No longer afraid of things to come, you welcome the unknown.
What is to be, in time will be.

Some things have gone by fast while others moved quite slowly.
Which direction to take? Sometimes you didn't know.
No matter what things may have transpired along the way, you are
    willing to see it through.
Where the road may lead, you just waited to see. You may had been
    already halfway there.
The roads may have been a little bumpy at times, then mellowed out
    for a much smoother ride, only to bring on a few twists and
    turns.

It was always okay to be a little concerned, but you didn't lose sight
    of what was just ahead.
You knew you'd never make it if every time you sensed a little fear,
    you'd pull over to side.
It seemed to work out very well to just take a deep breath and enjoy
    the ride.

Residual Effect

What the heck!
A couple of years gone by,
Sometimes, little reminders take me back,
I wonder why?
It's a damn residual effect.

A smell, a song, a movie, or a particular dish, to forget it is all I wish.
The sound of your voice, along with things you did, where I didn't
      have a choice

So f!@$ you!
Your deception and lies may creep into my head from time to time,
      but I will no longer let you cloud my mind and make my life
      a wreck.
The road forward has been a treacherous trek.
I'll continue to make my way through despite the residual effect.

Strength

You are beautiful inside and out.
You just need to take a moment, and you'll see it no doubt.
You have been dealing with a pain that was most unbearable.
It made you feel things that were not admirable.
You are a woman of faith and grace.
There is more to you than just a pretty face.
You have a wonderful heart, a warm smile, and always go the extra
    mile.
You will persevere despite anything you may fear.
You give your all and get back up every time you fall.

Sunshine after the Rain

As the early morning light made its presence known through the windows, she lay in bed with so many thoughts running through her head while he, hundreds of miles away, started his day feeling some sort of way.

Both thinking of how things had changed so quickly. It seemed a lifetime ago since their eyes last met (about 9,490 days to be somewhat exact).

She had gotten comfortable with how her life had been up to this point, and he had done the same. They had no idea that the friendship they had now would have such an impact on their lives.

They spent countless hours getting to know each other all over again. Sharing words of wisdom and encouragement. Talking about things from back in the day, current and past relationships, disappointments, times of enlightenment and excitement, followed by an occasional inappropriate slip.

At some point, things changed. It seemed to go to a place that neither had anticipated. They questioned what seemed to be getting more and more complicated.

Could this be a love story never to be told? They both had a desire for love based on respect, honesty, and trust. In each other, they had found all that and more.

The lives they had lived apart seemed to mirror in so many ways. They had dealt with so many ups and downs. For two people who had suffered so much, they had found in each other sunshine after the rain.

Missing What Has Never Been

Missing a passionate kiss that has never been shared
Missing a touch that has never been felt
Missing a hug that has never been embraced
Missing the long gaze into each other's eyes that has never been in focus
Missing the occasional playful moment that has never been acted on
Missing what we have that we've never had before
Missing memories that have never been made
Missing the day we will see each other again for the first time, anticipating in some way that I will be yours, and you'll be mine
Missing a love so real that's never been given
Missing what has never been, has only been possible because we have become more to each other than just friends

Occupant of My Mind

Dear occupant of my mind,

You have been a blessing and a much-welcomed surprise. This unexpected journey has really opened my eyes. It's unbelievable how quickly you stole my heart. When we are miles apart, it's truly amazing when you think about how this all came to be. The love I have for you and the love you have for me brings a vision of the future into focus so clearly. At a time when there is so much uncertainty, you have helped me see a more positive side of me. So occupant of my mind, I hope you will always stay. I wouldn't have it any other way.

Sincerely,
A very happy dwelling owner

Impatiently Waiting Patiently

A glimpse of what the future may bring has me looking forward to every morning.

Days filled with laughter and being loved are what makes a happily ever after. With each day that ends is one day closer to the moment it begins.

As we cross the threshold, we walk together where we will stay and love each other forever. So glad to have you in my life and excited to become your wife.

As we dance to love songs and the occasional old school rhyme, we know the wait was not a waste of time.

With everyday starting off right, by having each other in sight. No more distance between us, just enjoying a lifetime of happiness and trust.

So until then I will continue to love you unconditionally while impatiently waiting patiently for it all to begin.

I impatiently wait for it all to be true because there is not much meaning to my life if it's not being shared with you.

All in the Box

Arrival expected
Leaving no wonder
Lead to a love
I just now begun to understand
Nothing is perfect, but it comes pretty close
Trusting what is unknown
Has a way of revealing more curiosity
Each word said, held onto tightly
Believing what is and can be
Often wondering if it is really possible
Xoxo

The Little One

Test confirmed
Heartbeat sounds
Crackers and sprite, a new morning delight
Weeks pass, body grows
Too many trips to the bathroom to count
Months more, kicks felt
Cravings galore, feet sore
Clothes no longer fit
Backaches, tightening felt all around
Contractions coming more and more
Pain too strong to ignore
So much pressure, you're finally here
Chubby cheeks, tiny hands, and feet
Welcome to the world
Your journey's complete

Post

A lot has changed
Stretch marks, loose skin
Weight gained
Stomach cramping pains
Varicose veins
Breast tender, hope to soon look a little slender
Hair shedding, seen on the floor and bedding
Emotions unstable
For some reason, still craving apple pie
Bags under eyes, cellulite on thighs
Exhausted and sleep-deprived
To have a longer nap, this Momma has definitely tried

Little One Grows

Sleepless nights
3:00 a.m. cries
Diaper's wet
All dry, now back to bed
In a few weeks, sitting up
A cute giggle, tiny toes wiggle
Now, crawling across the floor
Don't touch that, now put that back
Little hands on everything
Almost two
Oh no, diaper's off
Now, time for the chase
So cute, spaghetti and sauce all over face
Bath time fun
Water splashing and bath toys
Hope for a peaceful night's sleep
Tomorrow, brings more joys

On Call

On call 24/7
A weekend off would be nice and to sleep in at least until ten
Kids get dressed
Running late, no time for breakfast
Grab a cereal bar, eat it in the car
Take them to school
Got to go here, drop this off over there
Take this down there
Oh no, forgot to stop in there
Kids need glue, projects due
Don't forget the grocery store
Don't have much, got to make it work
Kids have to be fed
Long lines, don't have much time
Wish there were two of me
No time for lunch, just grab some caffeine
Almost three, they'll be waiting for me
Back home, time to cook
Homework started, dinner's done
Dishes in sink, watch a show together
Time to relax, kids in bed
Such a long day
Thunderstorms loud
Now, everyone's in my bed
Woke up to one with a foot to my face
The other with her elbow pointed at my head
Seems crazy but I wouldn't have it any other way
It's only Wednesday

Adolescent

Complicated years yet to be discovered
Trying to fit in
Hoping to have lots of friends
Does this go with that, does that go with this
He said what
And she said that
But he's supposed to be with me
Always drama
Just want to have some fun
Try this with that
Take a sip of this
So much pressure
Is it really okay to be the only one that didn't
Will they notice if I hide
No plan of escape
Squeeze through the crowd and out the back
What was I thinking
Now, glad to be home

Breakfast

Grits or oatmeal
Oh no, a cereal spill
The dog begs for
Bacon and eggs
Juice sipped
Straw between lips
Forks against the plates clatter
It doesn't matter
Coffee's ready
Move steady
Started the day
Now, on the way

Slow Down

Busy, busy, busy.
What's the rush?
Take a moment and slow down.
You are not in a race to beat someone else.
Stop racing against yourself.
You'll make it there, wherever there maybe.
I know time may not wait for you, but you can make it work for
    everything you do.
Moving too fast, you can miss a lot.
Take some time to free you mind.
You may even remember some things you've already left behind.

Closet Noise

In the night, I heard a noise
From behind a slightly opened closet door
Something on the shelf has lost its balance
Nothing to be afraid of
Though soft, it was still quite a startling sound
Unstable bags and books
One slight shift was all it took

Scrolling

Sign in, page loading
Searching for what, not sure
Seeing what others have shared
New pics posted
Likes and comments made, keep scrolling
Is everyone really having such great lives
Pics and videos of family game night
Guys pranking their girlfriends, and Moms, that's just not right
Pets being mischievous
Pics of places everyone would love to go
Hacks and recipes shared multiple times, keep scrolling
Noticing a few negative post and insensitive comments
Fat-shaming, name-calling, racial and political views
Some live steaming and fake news
Challenges with things no one really wants to touch
Some happy moments, others not so much
Heated exchange of words leading to an online fight
Clap backs and prayer request
News reports of fires burning out west
Killer hornets, the new very deadly pest, keep scrolling
Uses for essential oils, and lists of planting soils
A new game invite and ways to treat a snake bite, scrolling on
You notice celebrities' links to multiple social media platforms
Chefs streaming live from their home kitchens
Making loaded nachos and Spatchcock chickens
Headlines about severe flooding and storms
COVID-19 and masks, WHO facing a great task
Lots of quarantine photos have become the new norm

Links to Zoom and Facebook rooms
Pic of bees sitting on flower blooms, scrolling stop
A very disturbing meme
You viewed a lot of content
Now, time to leave it be, you just saw something you wish you could
    unsee

Secrets Hidden in the Darkness

Secrets hidden in the darkness of night, reveal the true pain in the
  morning light.
Not sure how to embrace this new reality, every hour that passes
  seems to bring more uncertainty.

A true definition of beauty was what it once represented.
Even on the occasional bad day, a quick fix somehow found its way.
From full and thick, to thinning, to almost none; finding the perfect
  look seems impossible and certainly no fun.

Now almost all lost, self-esteem suffering is the cost.
Not much to be creative with, what more is there to do?

Dang it! Hair, I'm not ready to mourn you.

Thinning Days

What has happened to you?
You were always there.
I thought we made a perfect pair.
Whether curly, cut short, or spiked, you brought me compliments
    even when I didn't feel I looked all that great.

You made it through the almost-too-tight ponytail and styles with
    lots of gel.
No more occasional updo,
I'm left with limitations without you.

These thinning days are lasting a while.
It's getting harder to find my smile.
What a wondrous journey we had.
The thought of not having you anymore is making me very sad.
I'm really missing the relationship we once had.

Your Hue

Your complexion should never be a reason for rejection
Your hue is beautiful
Be confident, be proud
Your hue was made just for you
Love it the way it is
Own your shade, it is how you were made
It illuminates what's true
The color of your skin
Is not a sin
To everyone it is shown
Radiate happiness with that skin tone
You are a queen
You are a king
You own the scene
Haters can't change the script
It's just how you are equipped
Be proud to flaunt it
Because of it, you should never feel haunted
Rock it with grace, every inch up to your face
Your hue was made just for you

Ma

Strong and fierce,
Not sure if she had any worries or fears,
Never saw her upset or in tears.
She went to college to enhance her already acquired knowledge
She worked hard for the things she wanted to achieve
She even took a mechanics class.
She wasn't afraid to roll up her sleeve.
Dressed in coveralls and toolbox in hand, she was on her way to learn
about more than just the use of an oil pan.
Growing up, when things got tough, she always made sure we had
enough.
She shopped for the best deals and still made us great meals.
When there wasn't much, she would make peanut butter and crackers for lunch.
Dessert sometimes was a fundraiser candy bar.
Spaghetti always stretched quite far.
She made the sauce with fried ground beef, onions, and added little
water and tomato paste.
We loved it, nothing went to waste.
When things got really tough, hot dogs and beans found their way to
the scene, or beans and rice that were seasoned quite nice.
Being a single mom had its challenges, and yet she found a way to
manage.
When a door closed, she set new goals and embarked on a new path.

Momma A
L. Arrendale

Always thinking of her reassuring tone
Such powerful and encouraging words when things had gone wrong
She inspires and lifts you up
No matter what situation you find yourself in the middle of
She helps you rise above
Never seeming to be defeated
Always giving a prayer even when you didn't think you needed it

So caring and helpful
Her words full of power when spoken
A true angel with beauty and grace
To her, I give great praise

Much welcomed advice
So glad to have met her on this journey through life
Such an embodiment of support, confidence, and hope, many would
    say of this lady we call Momma A

The Grandmother I Used to Know

Alzheimer's or some other type of dementia, I was never really sure.
She spoke of things that were not real and of people no one knew.
Often in a state of confusion, somewhere between reality and an
   illusion,
Most times, not knowing what to do.
What happened to the grandmother I once knew?

For someone who got plenty of exercise, for her mind to go in such a
   way was quite a surprise.
As she got older, I noticed a change, the things she did and said came
   across as very strange.
Once a very strong and independent woman who always said she
   could do anything just as well or even better than any man.

She did her own gardening, mowed her own lawn, and lifted an ax,
   not only to chop wood but to kill a snake near where she stood.
No longer able to cook, bake, make quilts, or sew.
What happened to the grandmother I used to know?

She was always busy doing something, it seemed for most of the day,
   all while singing a gospel song. She'd call you out when you did
   something wrong. She'd be sure to let you know that was not
   the way to go. She'd often say, "Now, child, you know that ain't
   right. Don't do things out of spite."
She left many impressions with her words of wisdom.
What happened to the grandmother I used to know?
Where did she go?

Something in her mind had redirected her attention, bringing forth
   confusion in the words she would mention.
It was really hard seeing her that way.
The last few years of her life just didn't seem right. She was once a
   woman who was very spiritual and read her Bible every day.

What happened to the grandmother I used to know?
I had become someone she didn't recognize.
It was hard seeing the concern in her eyes.
Somehow, she had left before she was completely gone.

Multiple Scler-(what?)-rosis Struggling with MS

Multiple scler-what?
Can't let it kick my butt.
This disease, just like any other out there, definitely does not impress.
Some days, it's a struggle just to get dressed
Doctors say, get plenty of rest and reduce your stress.
As a mother, I say to myself, "Yeah right, good luck with that."
For this family of six, there are many meals to be fixed.
Struggling to lift a pan with my trembling hand or grip a knife.
What is the reason for this to happen in my life?
Feeling tired quite often, hoping they find a cure before,
This disease takes another person to a coffin.
Trying to take a walk, noticed balance is a little off.
Another MRI, new lesions on the brain, sometimes there's numb-
    ness, sometimes there's pain.
Doctors still say reduce your stress.
You know you're doing your best, but sometimes, you feel this will
    drive you insane.
On a good day, things are going your way, then you're quickly
    reminded,
When something as simple as putting on a shirt is hard to do.
You take your medicine as directed and hope that it will always be
    effective.
You may have this disease, but it doesn't have you.
(At least not yet)
Live everyday with no regret.

Stomach Issues and Food Allergies

Stomach issues, comfort of home much appreciated, plenty of bath-
room tissues
Public bath not a welcomed-walked path, courtesy flush a must.

Cramps from milkshake and burger with cheese brought me to my
knees.
Spinach, cabbage, and broccoli no more for me,
So much discomfort, bloating, and pain.

Sneezing, coughing, and drooling and wheezing, none of this is
pleasing.
Gluten, wheat, rye must say goodbye.
Avoid milk, nuts, and fish.
So many limitations, what else will create the perfect dish?

At restaurants, nerves on edge, no cross contamination they pledge
Fear of itchy throat, hives, and puffy face
Praying all is well with the first taste
No one wants an allergic reaction, but just in case, antihistamine and
EpiPen are nearby and ready for action

Acid reflux and heartburn, none of these issues are fun
This really sucks, everything wants to pick on the gut.
Many can relate when one or more of these things keep you up late.

A Night Out

My health is not the best, going out often feels like a test.
Don't want to get tired too quick or start to feel sick
I'm feeling confident now, but holding on to that, sometimes feels
    like a magic trick.
Shouldn't have to fake it, to make it.
Really want to rock this dress, don't want to look like a hot mess.
Being able to wear heels would be nice, but by the end of the night,
    these bunions are going to need ice.
So no heels, flats will have to do.
When a few sips of wine goes straight through, what's a lady going
    to do?
So I'll just skip the wine, and I'll be fine.
A night out is in great need, but what if to fatigue I have to concede.
Going to try to enjoy as much as possible.
Until my body says "That's it, you've had enough fun. I'm done."

Forgetting the Turmoil of the Day

During an evening walk, a slight breeze creates waves in the tall grass
    in the distance.
You admire the beauty while getting caught up in the wonderful
    smell of lavender growing nearby.
You stop for just a moment, as the warm evening sun hits your face,
    you close your eyes and can't imagine yourself any other place.
    Such a great way to end the day.

You suddenly feel bubbles tickling your nose and a draft across your
    toes.
You open your eyes, not too surprised, you are in a bubble-filled tub.
The warm bath and lavender oil have made your night.
Forgetting the turmoil of the day, the fragrance has taken it all away.

Comfort

Strong winds whip around the corners, heavy rain pounding the roof, this seems to be no concern to you.

Chili, simmering on the stove, is being stirred.
The aroma fills the house, blending with the smell of warm butter and sweet vanilla that arises from the cake you just baked, bring forth a feeling of comfort. No worries at all.

The rain begins to slow and the winds calm.
You sit down to enjoy a bowl of chili, accompanied by a glass of tea with ice and a slice of cake.
The chili's warming spices are quite nice.

Noticing the soft glow of flames from the fireplace just a few feet away, it doesn't bother you that it's a dreary day.
You realize how nice it is to have a moment to relax, while licking glaze off your fingers like you did when you were a kid.
Savoring every morsel of cake, having another slice shouldn't be a mistake.
Still raining outside, you don't even care, nowhere to be except right there.

Meditation

Close your eyes and clear your mind
(I have to go to the store but need to do laundry too)
Take a deep breath and clear your mind
(Maybe I'll start a load then go to the store, but wait, there are still
    dishes in the sink from last night)
Listen to your surroundings and clear your mind
Breathe in and out slowly, in and out, in and out
(I'll put the clothes in the dryer when I come from the store, then do
    the dishes)
Focus on that sound you're not sure what it might be.
(Is it water running, someone in a pool? Wait, there's no pool here)
Take a deep breath while focusing on the sound. Clear your mind of
    everything except the sound, slowly breathe out.
Deep breath in, slowly breathe out, breathe in slowly, breathe out
    slowly, focus on the sound
(Is someone continuously running water? Any more of this focusing
    and I'll have to go to the bathroom)
Now, just focus on your breathing in and out slowly, in and out, in
    and out, in and out.
Now, open your eyes.
(Feeling somewhat refreshed)
Oh, it's raining
(So that's what the sound was)

In Hindsight

In hindsight, I was so naïve.
Racism was written all over your sleeve.
You were way too cheerful, something told me to be careful.
You being despicable, I really didn't want to believe.
I quickly became aware that all your enthusiasm towards me was fake.
You treated me so unfair.
My encounters with you were a learning experience, not a mistake.
As I continue to look back, I realize you kept me around just to have me to talk about, I was your clown.
In conversations with others, I was the joke.
You thought I didn't hear you, but I did for sure, the last time you spoke.
Disgrace on your face, shown by the way you looked, like you ate something that had a bad taste.
Just because you're white and rich does not give you the right to call me a nigger bitch.
For so long, I thought you were a true friend, but from the beginning, it was all false.
I helped you out a lot and gave you advice, you said I was so nice.
Now I see, I was just someone you took advantage of.
I being an honest and trustworthy person is now your loss.

Black then Black Now

Hundreds of years of bloodshed
Hung, beaten, and shot dead
Slave sweat in the fields; songs sung throughout the hills
Given only scraps for meals
Women taken from their husbands
For the master's thrills
Beaten and slapped by their master's hands
Raped by slave masters over and over again
Gave birth to their babies in barns and pastures
How could anyone think this was a grand plan?
This I will never understand
Many fought to run away
Others, too afraid they'd be caught, chose to stay
Slavery ended but still not free
Still having to fight to live successfully
Riots and protests span many years
Mommas crying 'cause sons and daughters dying
Police brutality
Swept under the rug by some idiotic technicality
Being followed in the store, watched like a hawk
Down the street, just going for a walk
They say you got to be up to no good
This is not your neighborhood
Now in cuffs
Don't press your luck
"What is this about? That's my house, I just walked out."
They don't give a f—
This stuff happens way too many times

Even when no one has committed any crimes
Stream it live, to stop them from trying to hide evidence
How is what they are doing making any sense?
There is always something holding us back; things just keep getting
added to the stack.
Backs been against the wall, but now pieces of the stack are starting
to fall.

They Keep Missing the Point

The caravan is still on the move, hauling around bigotry, self-serving
    concepts, and superiority complexes
Leaving behind a deep wound
Complaints about their negative affects falls on deaf ears
Setting out to increase more fear

Opposing souls are tired of shedding tears
Many souls lost, too many to count
Hearts not filled with hate will breach their gate

The caravan holds tight to what it hauls, despite the many that dis-
    miss their calls
Peace, unity, acceptance, and inclusion is what the opposing souls
    want, but the caravan just keeps on hauling; missing the point
They just keep missing the point.

Your Racist Rant

With a hate-filled tone, you are quick to call us a derogatory name
and frequently say, go back to your country.
Thanks to your ancestors, we have no idea where this country you
speak of, maybe.
They brought our ancestors here and did whatever they wanted.
Now, this is our home.
Whether you like it or not, it's all we've got.
You, as descendants of your ancestors, don't have to continue their
racist ways.

Your racist rants are fueling the fires.
Generation after generation, you have suppressed our desires.
Burning down and blocking what we try to build.
There has been too much blood spilled.
You can say it is all a rumor, but there are so many things stolen from
us by you.

Your racist rants fuel our distress
You are the one making the big mess.
You say you're frustrated with us trying to douse the flame.
In all reality, no matter how you look at it, you are the one who is to
blame.
You claim we are not smart, but we notice your side-eye stare, and
the racist remark mumbled under your breath.

Wasting your energy on hate, while people of color could be the ones
you support and greatly appreciate.
Your racist rant said with great disgust, it is us you don't trust.

You take our ideas and say it was all you.
It is a damn shame because you really don't have a clue.
We just want to live peacefully with you.
You can evolve and help racism dissolve.
You have the ability to unlearn your racist ways.
We don't like the racist rants and lack of respect from day to day.
We will continue to pray and fight for better days.

When Calm Collides With Chaos

When all is calm, you are shown one side
In the middle of chaos, many other angles can no longer hide
When all is calm, you are in an area where things appear to be okay
But when chaos knocks at your door, there is calm no more
When there is chaos, you can see how life really is, whose hearts are
    in the right place to make the world a better living space
In the middle of chaos, you are able to see who is willing to extend
    their hands to help
You can see more clearly those who are out to destroy
Spewing all the hate they enjoy
When calm and chaos collide, those with evil agendas flaunt them
    with pride
Calm comes out even more fierce, with hopes to survive
To the evil, calm will not surrender.
It will just keep fighting on with hopes of one day being the victori-
    ous one.

The Place of the Reject

"You're a bright girl, but because you are black, you won't make it in this world," said by a white lady.

For me, hearing this just didn't seem right. It didn't make sense.

I always do my best, but still, I hear you're good, just not good enough.

Growing up, some girls with darker skin didn't want to be my friend.

"You're so light, you could pass for white," said by a dark-skinned girl.

"You can't be on our team."

I often wondered what that was supposed to mean.

As a little girl, I didn't understand why.

To have that mindset towards me, I felt great disrespect.

After becoming an adult, I, at times still, held the place of the reject.

"Wow! We're so impressed with your work, but unfortunately, you're over qualified. You should apply somewhere else that maybe a better fit for you," said by two white managers during an interview.

I think, wow, to my face they just lied.

There's a certain image they want to project, so once again I am holding the place of the reject.

Always Running Late, But Didn't Show Up At All

Our time is just as important as yours.
You are never on time, or you don't show up at all.
Your inconsideration for others does not win you any points.
You always have some new excuse for your time misuse.
You are never on time, or you don't show up at all.
You said you'd be there. We don't believe you care.
You missed the party the other day even though you claimed you
    were on your way.
You didn't even call.
You missed the school play on two different nights.
You said you fell asleep watching some televised fights.
You always have others waiting on you.
You said you'd be there in a few.
That was definitely not true.
You didn't show up at all.

The Drink You Seek

One that's shaken and not stirred
When you're feeling a bit perturbed
Maybe a scotch neat, or
A nice merlot served with some red meat
Tea or coffee served hot, flavored or not
Poured over ice on a hot summer day is nice
Sipped on the porch, or cuddled up inside
Ice cold lemonade that's freshly made
And sipped on while sitting the shade
Rosé, Moscato, or latte; whatever helps, make it a good day
A nice cold brew is waiting for you, or maybe you prefer
Bourbon on the rocks while you relax in your socks